Life - a journey.

The biker story

Kege

pencil

ISBN 978-93-5610-512-6

Published in India 2022 by Pencil

A brand of
One Point Six Technologies Pvt. Ltd.
123, Building J2, Shram Seva Premises,
Wadala Truck Terminal, Wadala (E)
Mumbai 400037, Maharashtra, INDIA
E connect@thepencilapp.com
W www.thepencilapp.com

Author biography

We all have gone through the phase of wondering what we should do with our life and always decide by thinking bout what society will say.

The 'rig-ma-roll' of making a career and setling down and making a family has always kept the pressure on us humans and we have all forgotten about LIFE....technically we are all breathing and living but none of us are Alive...we just live our daily routines and finally wither out and dissappear.

The same was the story of mine until one day i decided to stand up and forget bout what will people and society say or think and just decided to Live LIFE to its fullest and make every single day count and feel Alive in every breath i take...this is my journey from a regular guy to becoming totally different, from following the norms of society to braking them down and crushing them with my wheels, from a Chef to a professional Biker...yes you read it right..a biker..I was always fond of bikes and the sound of engines and thanks to Royal Enfield i get to live my LIFE every single day.

'LIFE IS SHORT SO DON'T WASTE IT JUST FIND WHAT MAKES YOU SMILE AND LEARN TO LIVE IT' - KEGAN

It all started when my heart and mind were not on the same page but since i was from a family so wound up by what society thinks and says, it wasn't easy to do what i wanted and just LIVE....so i was left with no choice but to just be secretive about my decisions and just do what i feel is right...and i went and gave the interview which changed my life forever and turned my passion into my profession..

My first day of my new life was to start in Chennai as i had to go to the Mecca of Enfield enthusiasts - The TVT RE Factory in Chennai. It wasn't easy and without the knowledge of my family i left for Chennai...initially it wasn't easy to convince my parents and siblings of the career altering choice have made but over a period of time they realised that this is what i want although at times i feel that my mum still is apprehensive to the path i choose...but one thing I've learnt in life is never ever regret the decisions one takes as long as its taken on your own without any pressure from anywhere.

'Forget the past as it is footprints in sand- they will vanish with the wind, Dont worry about the future- it is unpredictable like the weather, Just enjoy the present - its the only thing that matters and is actually real.'

- Kegan

So without any more boring gyan lets just get into the adventures and misadventures of my 'LIFE! - THE JOURNEY '

CONTENTS

The first 500

It all started as a regular day getting ready for work when all of a sudden my mum who was in Goa with the rest of my family called to check on me and told me that they all are missing me a lot. It was then that i decided to surprise them…but the question was how do i reach Goa
It was as if like an angel my bike the Royal Enfield Classic 350 smiled at me saying

Ride Me..

At first i was a bit nervous as i had never ever gone for such a long trip all alone and that to on a bike and to add to the dilemma was the fact of not knowing the route to Goa. But i guess the excitement of being with my family and the adventure of riding my bike all in all gave me the courage to go ahead with the ride. So i packed up a few clothes and the bare essentials in my trusty old backpack, wore my riding gear and locked the house door and got ready to ride. Leaving the house at 12:30 in the afternoon wanting to reach my destination as early as possible.
As i started the engine, the roar of it made my heart race and got my adrenaline pumping. Soon it was as if like magic the bike's engine beat was synchronized to my heartbeat, and so i rode with my cellphone's GPS on and only adventure on my mind.

As i started off towards my first obstacle the Katraj Ghat i realised that i have to fill up fuel and so my first stop about 5km from home was the gas station. I filled my tank full paid the guy and got ready to ride once again and off i went.

As i cleared the ghat section hoping that my bike doesn't give me any trouble the only thing playing on my mind was what would my Mom say if she knew what i was upto.

After the Ghats came the best part of the journey the Bombay- Bangalore highway, a beautiful four lane road with nothing but greenery on both sides "The Ideal Road". As i kept on riding not realising that my mobile charge had gone leaving me without a GPS to follow. Luckily the road was well tagged having milestones with directions at regular intervals. As i was nearing Kholapur around 4 in the evening i started to feel hungry and was on the look out for a place to eat and give my bike and myself some much needed rest as we both were riding continuously for the past 4 1/2 hrs.. But to add to the fact that i was hungry all the restaurants were closed due to dusherra festival. So with an empty stomach i continued to ride hoping to find something open soon. At around 5pm just before Nipani i spotted a small joint and stopped there for lunch. After a good meal and some rest i asked the waiter for directions and continued my adventure. As i neared my next obstacle the Amboli ghat it had started to turn dark and made me wonder if i made the right decision of riding to Goa, nevertheless it was to late to turn back now and i kept riding ahead entertaining myself by singing my favorite songs inside my helmet feeling good bout myself. Not to my surprise the Amboli ghat had real bad roads and riding through it avoiding the potholes as much as i can trying to avoid a puncture was a task in itself. But finally after a long stressful part of the ride i saw the sign 'ghat over' made me happy and its there where i met the 'Yamaha mission 10000 riders' who were all regrouping and waving out to me as i passed by acknowledging me as one of them a 'Rider' it felt real good.

A few kms away i had to make a small pitstop to answer nature's call and as the riders i met before passed by the ride captain stoped and asked if i was ok and wanted to join them for the rest of the ride. As i accepted the invitation and started riding with them for the last part of the journey the Sawantwadi ghat and then into Goa it was already around 8pm. We had to clear the ghat with lights on. As i rode with the boys from mission 10000 i learnt a few more riding safety tips when in a group. "Thank you mission 10000 riders". As we entered goa it was around 9 pm and as i bid farewell to my new friends i wished them a safe ride and headed off towards my home and family.

As i reached home my family was down by the poolside and when they saw me they all were excited and awestruck and couldn't believe i made the trip on bike all alone. My older brother was so happy that he congratulated me on my achievement and then went on to say "i am jealous of you" in a loving way. Mum on the other hand had a totally different approach and kept touching me to see if i was really there.

The highlights of the ride were

– my bike didn't give me any trouble

– for major portion of the ride the roads were beautiful.

– the experience was great and made me grow as a person and a rider.

The ride back home
After the long enjoyable ride into Goa and spending a good fun filled weekend with family here, it was time to head back to the daily routine of life in Pune. This time being accompanied by my whole family in the car as i ride along. But the major dilemma was which route to take. As the Gaganbawda and Amboli ghats were only potholes. So the only next option was the Chorla ghat. It was a new road for all of us hence we were a bit reluctant to use it, but after some research and with the help of Google maps we decided to go with it.

And so the journey begins….

After a good nights sleep and a quick check of the bike, we left from our home in Goa at 6:30 am. heading for Chorla ghat. Our first stop was for fuel not very far from home.
As i rode through the village roads of North Goa i was overwhelmed by the amount of cattle on the road due to which i was forced to ride slowly.
The first ghat section was amazing. It was an intoxicating mix of nature's wonders in all its beauty and a really smooth and wide road. To add to the mix was zero traffic.
After this mesmerizing ride through the forest the ghat opens up into Belgaum city which was a bit busy but the good roads more than made up for it. This is where i had my second stop and had a nice breakfast of puri bhaji and a exceptionally good coffee. After the 'pet puja' it was time to hit the road once again.
Once out of Belgaum city we hit the Bangalore – Mumbai highway and as before it was a pleasure to ride on..
It was around 2pm when we made are stop for lunch at a

McDonald's near Kholapur, and after a quick bite and a small visit to the men's room i was ready to ride all the way home not knowing what is in store up ahead for me. As i neared Shirval we ran into some rain, this is when my bro Ryan called me up and informed me bout the heavy rain on the ghat section. So i handed over my bag to him and for the first time rode without any luggage. At first it felt like something missing but as i got into the riding groove i tackled the ghat as if it was my daily road to work. It was fun but i still missed the Chorla ghat and all its beauty.
It was then when it struck me that in a few more kilometers my adventurous road trip will come to an end and that made me a bit sad but at the same time a feeling of pride and self accomplishment crept in knowing that i had finished a 1000 kms journey all alone on my bike. It was fun and has kept me wanting for more.

Highlights of the ride
– My bike kept up to its tag line "built like a gun" and didn't give me any trouble throughout the trip.
– My family acknowledged the fact that i am a rider and can ride long distances.
– Proved to myself that i can ride long distances.
– Have a feeling of pride and self accomplishment and has inspired me to write this blog.

To finish off all i can say is that the ride was complete in every way possible and has increased my appetite to ride ten fold.
Will keep on updating this blog with my future ride experiences and hopefully some more pictures too.

Until the next ride….keep thumping…..

All in all it was a good day and an even better ride

The ride back

After the long enjoyable ride into Goa and spending a good fun filled weekend with family here, it was time to head back to the daily routine of life in Pune. This time being accompanied by my whole family in the car as i ride along. But the major dilemma was which route to take. As the Gaganbawda and Amboli ghats were only potholes. So the only next option was the Chorla ghat. It was a new road for all of us hence we were a bit reluctant to use it, but after some research and with the help of Google maps we decided to go with it.

And so the journey begins….

After a good nights sleep and a quick check of the bike, we left from our home in Goa at 6:30 am. heading for Chorla ghat. Our first stop was for fuel not very far from home.
As i rode through the village roads of North Goa i was overwhelmed by the amount of cattle on the road due to which i was forced to ride slowly.
The first ghat section was amazing. It was an intoxicating mix of nature's wonders in all its beauty and a really smooth and wide road. To add to the mix was zero traffic.
After this mesmerizing ride through the forest the ghat opens up into Belgaum city which was a bit busy but the good roads more than made up for it. This is where i had

my second stop and had a nice breakfast of puri bhaji and a exceptionally good coffee. After the 'pet puja' it was time to hit the road once again.
Once out of Belgaum city we hit the Bangalore – Mumbai highway and as before it was a pleasure to ride on..
It was around 2pm when we made are stop for lunch at a McDonald's near Kholapur, and after a quick bite and a small visit to the men's room i was ready to ride all the way home not knowing what is in store up ahead for me. As i neared Shirval we ran into some rain, this is when my bro Ryan called me up and informed me bout the heavy rain on the ghat section. So i handed over my bag to him and for the first time rode without any luggage. At first it felt like something missing but as i got into the riding groove i tackled the ghat as if it was my daily road to work. It was fun but i still missed the Chorla ghat and all its beauty.
It was then when it struck me that in a few more kilometers my adventurous road trip will come to an end and that made me a bit sad but at the same time a feeling of pride and self accomplishment crept in knowing that i had finished a 1000 kms journey all alone on my bike. It was fun and has kept me wanting for more.

Highlights of the ride
– My bike kept up to its tag line "built like a gun" and didn't give me any trouble throughout the trip.
– My family acknowledged the fact that i am a rider and can ride long distances.
– Proved to myself that i can ride long distances.
– Have a feeling of pride and self accomplishment and has inspired me to write this blog.

To finish off all i can say is that the ride was complete in every way possible and has increased my appetite to ride ten fold.
Will keep on updating this blog with my future ride experiences and hopefully some more pictures too.
Until the next ride….keep thumping….

90 kms to breakfast

90kms to breakfast" if a normal person heard this they would think I am crazy and have totally lost it, but for 200 bikers this was just another fun day in the sun.

This time round i rode with a large group of avid bikers and a very close friend for breakfast. Got up at 6am got ready and left for the rendezvous point. All this only to have some Chai-Pakoda.

After a quick brief about the event by the organisers "IBW" we were all set to ride to Supa about 90 km from Phoenix mall on nagar highway.

People actually stopped what ever they were doing only to stare at the 200 bikers out for breakfast on a Sunday. It was a wonderful feeling and a sight never to be forgotten.

After a good long ride on the beautiful nagar highway we reached our destination Kamat hotel in Supa. To see all the bikes parked in a line was totally mesmerizing. The IBW did a great job in welcoming all the riders both veterans and amateur. After a good breakfast and a nice hot cup of masala chai the fun started. First it was a KTM Duke that did a whellie and then followed by other Duke's doing different stunts. Then came the big boys with their big engines making music with the sound of the exhaust. All in all it was fun and exciting. But wats a party if the bulls don't make noise and so with all the masti in us both me n Sarde took our bikes to the centre and let the beast loose

and made all the noise possible enough to silence a Hyabusa.
Before we left the venue all the riders were given a biker patch, my first ever stating "i rode mine to IBW"
It was fun and a great experience.

Ride to the Garden of the Gods

It was all of a sudden when a friend of mine called me up and said lets go for a ride.

So the very next early summer morning we left for a place called as KAAS its a small hill top on the Western Ghats of Maharashtra also known as The valley of flowers.

The ride to the top was unforgettable and unnerving due to the steep winding roads covered in dense fog. It gave the illusion of riding through the clouds to Olympus- the place of the Gods.

Once at the destination the view was all so breathtaking as the fog cleared and revealed the beauty of nature in all its versitality and veracity with different coloured flowers across the plateau with ponds and small streams crossing the path reminded me of a perfect painting of all things good and beautiful. The place as a different type of aura around it that calms you down and makes you forget all your worries and just live in the moment and be happy. It was like i visited the Garden of the Gods….i was blessed to witness such beauty and for me the place has left a lasting impression on my soul and will never be able to forget it. I recommend everyone should visit KAAS at least once to just be enlightened.

Ride to the city of Palaces

This was by far my longest solo ride till date. The journey was full of excitement and a stepping stone in my path of becoming a seasoned biker.
The route for the trip was simple from Pune to Bangalore and from there to Mysore with a stop at the ranganatittu bird sanctuary a must visit for all nature lovers and bird watchers alike.
In this journey of mine the gear i purchased from rynox was a boon and i must say not only is the gear reasonably priced but its totally durable and looks beautiful as well.
After a hearty breakfast at home and loading "El Torro" my bike the classic 350 i started my ride at around 6:45am. Having done the Bangalore trip before i decided to do a two stop ride to Bangalore. The roads are beautiful only thing to look out for is the wind blast you get when a truck passes by. But thanks to the bulls weight i was pretty safe from this wind effect. The ride to Bangalore was good i reached safely without any trouble or tantrums from my bull which the Enfields are notoriously known for.touch wood.
The ride to mysore was much more scenic and had some twisted roads, highways and a bit of off road fun as well. On the way i passed through the wooden toy city and sugar city. I even managed to get a speeding ticket on the highway, my first ever. Before reaching mysore city being

the nature lover i am i decided to take a small detour to visit the well known Ranganatittu bird sanctuary- a beautiful natural eden where hundreds of different species of birds both indigenous and migratory can be seen along with a few crocodiles that inhabit the lake that the sanctuary sits around. A must visit for everyone. Its a place that will make you fall in love with life and nature alk over again. After my little detour into nature i got back on track to reach mysore city and my humble abode for the night Hotel Ginger. After unloading the bike and taking a quick yet much needed shower and a hot cup of coffee i was ready to do some sightseeing and landed the brindavan gardens all though it was not what i hoped it would be i have to say the ride to the gardens was great.
Back to the hotel and a nice dinner i hit the bed for much needed rest. The next day i headed out to fullfill my hunger for nature and found my way to the Mysore zoo. It was an experience to cheerish being able to see animals such as the giraffe, ape, rhyno, zebra, anacondas, wallaby, different kinds of birds an all the big cats was simply amazing. To add to it they are all uncaged and in a natural habitat.
After fun with nature it was time to go back in time and visit the Mysore palace, i must say if history was this interesting when i was a kid id come first in class.
Anyways after a good weekend full of fun and learning it was time to head back home.
As with all my previous rides even this one has thaught me something and increased my appetite to ride.
For all my rider buddies who are starting on their biker path id like to say " respect the road and your bike, you will enjoy the journey even more"..its not how fast you get

there but its about how much u enjoyed getting there…
Keep thumping….

The Jungle trails of Goa

It's been a while since I last wrote, mainly because of the absence of my motivation, my heart, my Bagad Billi who also was my proof reader and most honest critic. But life goes on and if only as a distraction from all the pain I have started to write again.

This time it's all about a one day excursion into the jungle trails of Goa.

It was a nice sunny day even though it was the beginning of monsoons but lucky for us the skies were clear. The ride started from Varca and went through a series of off-road paths on the bank of a canal. It was a pleasure to ride with my colleague Arjay who was on a Himalayan, I on the other hand was riding the all new Trials 500 and was enjoying every moment of it. The scenery was all green with a few peacocks around. After a short tea break we moved on to the second leg of the ride and entered the Netravali forest reserve.

It was a narrow uphill trail with beautiful Twisties and steep inclines. Navigation through the trail was a task but we were determined to finish the trail. The only place we both got stuck was on a steep incline full of slippery stones, it took us a few extra minutes but we managed to get the bikes through. Before we could exit Netravali forest we had a small stream to cross and then flat grasslands before the final exit gate.

This was not the end of the trail as we still had to cross the Kali Tiger reserve which was situated on the Goa Karnataka border. 70kms away from the exit one of the bikes got a puncture. We somehow managed to get the bike to the exit slipping and sliding. All in all it was a good day. An adventure I will never forget.

Riding the coast

This was the first ride on my brand new Interceptor 650 a.k.a Bagad Billi.

I rode down from Pune through the beautiful scenic and not so smooth roads of tamini Ghat to Mahad, as this was the quickest way to reach the west coast.

From Mahad onwards the roads were smooth and winding, perfect for testing the bikes performance. I must say that she handles like a dream.

Somewhere on the western ghats just before we could hit the coastal road is where I fell truely in love with my bike and the way she rides. Simply put the Interceptor 650 is a 'beautiful beast.'

During the ride there were a lot of first for the Bagad Billi. First time on the coast, first ferry ride and first time on the beach. We had a blast together on the ride. Its time's like these which make me realize how lucky I am to have the job I have. There is something about riding a bike which just feels right and no matter what pain one is going through just go out on the bike and let the ride heal you.

Life is a lot like a ride, there are good roads, bad roads, good weather, bad weather but you don't give up the ride because of these reasons, then why should you give up on life when things go south. Remember as all good things come to an end, all bad things too . All you need to do is hold on and believe that voice in your heart which says to carry on. When in life you hit a bad patch just drop a gear and slow down. The fastest way to clear a bad road is by slowing down.

This is what riding a bike has thought me and it's only my bikes that have got me through some of my most hardest days and even till date it's only because of my bikes that I am still sane.

Ride - de - Daman

It's a long time since I wrote about one of my many journeys but I guess this one is worth a try.so this is how it went...

It was a ride organised by BRC, pune the club that I ride with and since I hadn't ridden with them for some time so I decided to join it..The ride was to Daman with a stop over in Dhanu...so as usual I got up late and was the last one to reach at the assembly point on Friday early morning and as soon as briefing was over we rode out all 21 Royal Enfield roaring on the empty streets of pune. Before we new it we had hit the highway and the roars turned into loud thunderous sounds....that's the beauty of this beast...it knows when to purr..and when to roar..

Anyways after a couple of hours we made our first Pitstop for breakfast, having little knowledge that this was only the beginning of a series of stops before we reach Dhanu..at times it was annoying since am used to riding nonstop for long distances and stopping every 50-75kms Was just not my style..Anyways after a pep talk with one of my fellow riders I was calm and decided to ride in the second last position helping out the sweep and throttling up once in a way...The road till mumbai was open and fun to ride but on entering Mumbai the true feeling of a traffic jam kicked in with bumper to bumper traffic and no where to go we crawled ourselves out of Mumbai and once again hit the highway.. This time an even better road greeted us with a beautiful scenery from time to time and some village roads and to top it of a nice stretch of off road helped refresh everyone...finally we reached Dhanu and after a tasty lunch an a much needed wash we decided to hit the beach but with our bikes trying to do some beach sand bashing...This is where my bull decided to start acting up and got stuck in the sand not willing to budge..After lot of trying and pulling and pushing all to no avail we finally had to pick her up out of the sandy bed she made for herself...I have to say it was a lot of fun even though we ended up getting sand on ourselves. .

Next morning was the ride to Daman and I must say the roads were beautiful and got a chance to finally open up the full throttle on my bull. Here to we had some fun and enjoyed ourselves...

The ride back I did a solo run and rode nonstop from Daman to Lonavala where I stopped for lunch after a good meal began my journey back home reaching pune within a total time of 5 hours..all in all the ride was good and thought me a few more things in group riding..

Hope you enjoy reading it....Ride hard Ride Safe..

NH4

After the ride to goa and supa i was all charged to ride to Bangalore but didn't have a reason until a few months ago when my older brother and bhabi shifted there.
The Bangalore ride was always playing on the back of my mind but was never certain about doing it.
But opportunity always favours the brave and soon my entire family went to visit my brother. Me left all alone at home with only my bike and a warning from my mother that if i come on bike to Bangalore she will sell it.
So after a lot of thinking and pondering about the issue i decided to put everything on the line and face the consequences and ride.
The mix of wanting to see one's family and the urge to ride can be a deadly combination almost like an electric charge that keeps you going and makes you do things you wouldn't normally.
The next day i left early at around 7 am i hit the NH7 but this time i was totally geared up and started to ride. The weather was cold and even after wearing my jacket it was unbearable, so after Karad i decided to stop for breakfast and wait there till the weather gets a bit warm.
After some chai and misal pav and after getting warmed up i got back on the saddle and began to ride. The ride on a whole was beautiful and scenic, a must do for all young avid beginner riders. As you enter into Karnataka all you

see on either side are coconut and supari trees a beautiful sight.

I was very happy riding on the highway but once i entered Bangalore the traffic was bad. All in all it was a great experience and a good learning.
Another chapter to my rider life.

Back to base
After a well deserved vacation with my family full of fun, adventure and an unforgettable puncture it was now time to say adiós to the garden city of Bangalore and head back to life daily routine. So i gassed up my bike, did a electrical check and called it a night as i had to leave early at 6:30 am the next morning.
In the morning all geared up i saddled my bike, said a small prayer and said goodbye to family and Bangalore city. As i hit the highway i was free and began to let the beast loose. My first stop was Sira where i had my breakfast..nothing much just a packet of biscuits and some road side chai. After the break i got back on the saddle and hit the road once again.
After riding nonstop for bout 4 hours i had to stop as my stomach was growling and reminding me that it was time for lunch. So i haulted at the nearest exit near Haveri and had a couple of protein bars and some juice, clicked a few pics and after a few minutes got back on my bull.
As i wanted to clear the ghat section before it gets dark i kept riding continuously not forgetting to admire natures beauty along the road. But at around 4pm i made my last stop in Nipani for some tea. After that it was a long ride

home and it felt longer as i reached closer to pune. As i finally reached home i had a feeling of accomplishment and same time felt sad coz my ride was over.
This ride has only left me wanting for more. Will be planning my next ride soon.
Till then cheers...and....keep thumping.....

www.ingramcontent.com/pod-product-compliance
Lightning Source LLC
LaVergne TN
LVHW100339181026
850499LV00039B/1141
9789356105126